Mother and Daughter Reflections

Mother and Daughter Reflections

A Celebration of a Special Bond

PAT ROSS 1943-

**Andrews McMeel
Publishing**

Kansas City

Book composition by Holly Camerlinck

00 01 02 03 TWP 10 9 8 7 6 5 4 3 2 1

Library of Congress Cataloging-in-Publication Data:

Ross, Pat, 1943-
    Mother and daughter reflections : a celebration of a special bond / Pat Ross.
        p.   cm.
    ISBN 0-7407-0499-0 (hardcover)
    1. Mothers and daughters. 2. Mothers and daughters—Pictoral works. I. Title.
    HQ755.85.R666 2000
    306.874'3'0222—dc21   99-055090

Andrews McMeel books are available at quantity discounts with bulk purchase for educational, business, or sales promotional use. For information, please write to: Special Sales Department, Andrews McMeel Publishing, 4520 Main Street, Kansas City, Missouri 64111.

With love to my daughter,
Erica Hope Ross

Hope is the thing with feathers
That perches in the soul . . .
And sings the tune without words
And never stops . . . at all

— EMILY DICKINSON
1830–1886

The author with her daughter at age four in 1976.

Preface

For more years than I care to admit, whenever I tried to unravel the many issues involved in being a mother of a daughter, I encountered an endless ball of yarn. Sandwiched between two significant female forces—my mother and my daughter—I'd managed to convince myself that I had Mother Matters under control. During the time when I was taking such relationships for granted, I'd have been hard-pressed to reflect on my own personal story with much insight. Then came a sharp wake-up call that would change always my grasp of this powerful generational loveknot.

My great-grandmother is a vague and tragic legacy. She died only months after giving birth to her fifth child. Four children were sent to live with relatives. Baby Jennie was raised by her Victorian father and a demanding "Aunt" Rose, the housekeeper.

The part of the story that's become a family fable is how, one day, Jennie heard the neighborhood children talking about their mothers. Bewildered, Jennie went home and asked, "Don't I have a mother, too?" That saddened child went on to become a nurturing grandmother—my beloved "Nanny." And yet there was always something missing in my grandmother's soul which made her less than confident in the world than those daughters who have been wanted, loved, sustained, and prized by a mother.

This motherless theme was destined to be carried into the next generation when my grandmother found herself on her own with two small daughters. At the age of six, my mother, Anita, was left in the care of assorted women relatives, who had problems and children of their own, while her working mother stood long hours behind the dazzling retail counter of a Baltimore silver maker. With too little means and too hard a struggle, my proper and dutiful grandmother must have seen her mothering role as a luxury—indeed, the illusive myth of her own childhood—as well as something for the leisure class.

Interestingly, one of Mother's most tender recollections of her own mother's love is the clean school uniform she found laid neatly across the bottom of her bed every morning in a house where they shared a room. The familiar Catholic school blue cotton dress and apron had been washed, starched, and ironed to perfection long after others' bedtimes. Her self-respecting Irish mother was determined that her daughter would not be considered a neglected charity case. Perhaps to please such a distracted and proud parent, Anita became the nuns' poster child—the winsome and independent surrogate daughter of many aunts and sitters who filled in the gaps of motherhood. Mother may have spent her life longing for an attentive full-time mother who starched and ironed more out of love than of pride, yet I believe she developed into an empathetic person because of the variety of her caregivers—some kind and generous, others indifferent and cruel—and because of the sheer quantity of mother figures who touched her life.

When I came along, Mother became a full-time mother in the most devoted sense of the term. By the time my sister, Jeanne, arrived four years later, Mother had thrown herself into the task of raising her daughters with grateful abandon. Though we sisters often strayed from the ideal, Mother insists that being a mother has been the greatest joy of her life.

It took many years for me to look back at my own childhood and realize just how lucky I was to have a mother like that—one who dropped everything when my throat felt like fire to whip up a healing glass of orange juice folded into sweetened and stiffened egg whites with finely crushed ice; who taught me to make a blue-ribbon apron for the 4-H fair; who was never too busy or preoccupied to drive me everywhere, encourage me to talk things out, listen to my dreams, encourage my creativity, and troubleshoot with ideas whenever I whined, "What can I do now, Mommy?" Dreaded boredom—it was a state both of us steadfastly avoided, and Mother knew all the tricks.

Of course, there were times when I wanted someone else's more calm and collected mother—a mother who wouldn't dash around her daughter's camp cabin only seconds before the other girls arrived, testing and bouncing on all eight mattresses to make certain I got the best one; a mother who—at the many local public-speaking contests I entered—wouldn't lip-synch my entire speech from the back of the darkened room while I gripped the podium, feeling alternately supported and mortified.

Mother's energy and love were inexhaustible, but, eventually, they exhausted me. Since it was hard to find shortcomings to criticize, I decided to find fault with her doing too much. My adolescent phrases sounded more like those of a stubborn two-year-old: "Stop it!" and "Leave me alone!" as well as the all-occasion "*Pleeze*, Mother!"

I gorged on cream-filled doughnuts, buttered corn bread, and hot fudge sundaes at the local Tasty Freeze in a small southern town where I attended boarding school. Soon I'd gone up several sizes, yet Mother continued to insist I was "beautiful." I hated my healthy-looking apple cheeks, the tight blouses that I dared not tuck in, and my mother's total blindness to fat. Most of my new mother figures at school were proper and intimidating educators bent on expanding my mind. I was caught between unconditional praise and achievement-dependent evaluation.

Mother with me in June 1943. I was called Patsy then.

As I grew into adulthood and needed an independent life, Mother found it difficult to let me go; but, because she knew me well, she transformed herself into my true champion, helping me pack up my cozy mauve-colored room with the ruffled voile curtains, paving the way for my departure from my father as well, an inflexible man who had little understanding of a creative upstart like me. Leaving my mother in the dust of small-town life, I fled to New York City and worldly ways. I found no lack of criticism there. Yet no matter how far I'd run geographically, I continued to pick up the phone to close the distance, especially when a siren screamed tragedy and loneliness from the city street below, just to make sure my mother was still there for me.

Over the years, my style with my mother became more direct and confrontational than with the other people in my personal life. Consequently, the relationship became more comfortable for both of us. The catalyst for this change was the Boursin Cheese Incident. Mother was promoting a new cheese with her usual intensity and I was resisting with my usual stubbornness. I remember Mom saying something like, "Try it! It's something new called Boursin," and tempting me with a tidbit to my mouth, as though I were two years old. Predictably, I shot back: "Mother, I *know* what Boursin is and I'm just not hungry!" That did it. "You New Yorkers think you're so sophisticated!" Mother snapped, removing the cheese tray and her indignity to the kitchen.

Mother with my younger sister, Jeanne, and me on the Chesapeake Bay in the early 1950s.

After the weekend, I bought a copy of Nancy Friday's *My Mother, My Self*, which seemed written expressly for me. The book confirmed what I felt; that I needed more distance from this person who was uncomfortably like myself. The following week, I had my hair cut by a new stylist who certainly had never laid eyes on my mother. Yet, ironically, I wound up with a haircut that was a carbon copy of hers, fluffy bangs and all. Or was I the only one who saw her face, her hair, in the salon's large and revealing mirror? After that, I withdrew entirely to a minimum of formal contact with my mother. On Hallmark occasions, I'd look for the most mindless card on the rack, slap on a stamp, and wait to hear the corner mailbox clank the completion of my obligation.

In between the time I'd established my independence from home and my separateness from my mother, I saw myself as starting a new generation of women when I gave birth to a daughter with whom I was determined to do everything differently. Or so I thought. However, having a daughter rendered me vulnerable as well as blessed from both sides of my genetic heritage.

Mother, who had long since registered my angry message, retreated and rarely called. No longer was I able to groan to myself at her predictable greeting: "This is just a quick call," knowing full well that such a call would be very unlikely. The less I heard from her, the more I began to wish for any length of call—Mom asking me to listen to her latest short story or haiku verse before the writer's group met; telling me about a new wonder vitamin I ought to be taking or a way to stop my daughter from digging at the tiny chicken pox bumps on her perfect small face.

At the end of an especially stressful week—dicey politics at the office,

My mother, Anita, with her mother in the mid-1950s.

house-keeper on medical leave, a temporary baby-sitter who was winning over my child with pancakes in the shape of Mickey Mouse ("Mommy, why don't *you* ever make me pancakes with Mickey ears?"), a stack of past-due bills, a broken washing machine, a husband on business abroad—I wondered what my mother would do in such a situation. Suddenly, I realized that not only did I miss her, but I missed her *interest* in me. Above all, I missed her unconditional love.

The mending began gradually and without apologies, for who could explain precisely why my mother and I had come to that standoff? At the end of this transition, our personal distance could be seen as a kind of gift. Mother had yielded to my rebellion; consequently, I was beginning to lean in her direction. Finally, we were ready to see each other in new ways and start again. Mother was never able to get to that point of reconciliation with her mother. They danced around the real issues of their relationship till the day Nanny died.

My birth—as the first grandchild in the family—found Nanny's life serene and protected in a second marriage with a man who'd loved her secretly since grade school. Blessedly, I was not another responsibility to shoulder at that point in her life; not another struggle to overcome. I could be her joy. So, from the beginning, I formed a sustaining bond with my petite grandmother, whose grip of steel made strong men strain to get the lid off the mayonnaise jar.

When I was a child, Nanny would say, "Come keep me company while I cream my face." I'd perch on a chair next to her dressing table and watch Nanny go through her Ponds ritual, fascinated as, rhythmically, she massaged the rich white cream into her velvet complexion, then up and down her neck in an undulating upward motion, finally sweeping any excess cream onto her shoulders and down to every fingertip.

While we waited for the cream to work its wonders before she tissued it off, Nanny was an especially good listener. The total appreciation and non-judgmental acceptance I felt in her presence made Nanny my confidante for life. Many years later, the women in our family constitute four generations of dedicated face creamers, and I rarely remove my makeup without appreciating how a womanly ritual has become a sustaining memory.

"You should do your next book about mothers and daughters," my editor suggested at the time I was completing *A Circle of Enduring Love*, the companion book to *The Kinship of Women*. It was such a natural subject for this line of books that, already, I'd begun to pick up irresistible old photos of mothers and daughters at antique paper and photo shows. With little conscious effort on my part, the most heartwarming images seemed to beckon to me. I tucked them away in a shoe box and waited. "Yes," I replied, "but not now. Not yet." I knew my heart would be too invested in such a project, and for that very reason I was trying to keep a safe distance from the subject of mothers and daughters.

One day, in an ironic blow of fate, my adult daughter had flared like a kitchen match and separated her life from mine. Suddenly, I was every mother's second-worst nightmare—a daughterless mother. It was a painful reminder of my own separation from my mother those many years before. When I confided in a friend who had lost a daughter by death—truly the *worst* and most unfathomable nightmare—she consoled me by offering, "It *is* a death of a sort, but unlike me, you have hope always." Hope—that was my daughter Erica's middle name, chosen by her ardent feminist mother of the '70s whose visions of the future did not include the possibility of rejection.

"Give her time," my mother advised wisely. "She needs her space without being in your shadow. Send her a card or drop her a note to let her know you're there. But otherwise, back off and stop being so impatient to make things happen." And so I took my mother's good advice, but mostly because I had little choice. The months turned into a year, then two years . . .

Once, I broke down in the cereal section of a supermarket—right in front of the bright yellow boxes of Erica's favorite Cheerios, taking a few shoppers and a stock boy by surprise. At home, I could no longer endure hearing Judy Collins sing the heartrending "The Rest of Your Life," and sent the entire album to the Siberian top shelf. On Mother's Day, I'd remember red paper hearts cut large and lopsided, the gift of a flamboyant green scarf woven at camp that I kept promising to wear, a tiny clay house inscribed to me that I'd chipped in a careless moment. Suddenly, I regretted I'd taken these treasures so much for granted. Sometimes, I found myself trying to mother some of the young women in my life—from editorial assistants to the daughters of friends. But none of

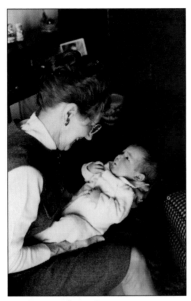

My grandmother, Jennie, with Erica in 1972.

them came close to filling the void or kindling the irreplaceable bond I'd made with my own daughter.

Sometimes I'd be overcome by a keen sensory awareness of my daughter: her flowing substantial hair with its wholesome fragrance of fresh shampoo and its jet-black sheen; her skin the texture of fine velvet (with such similarity to my grandmother's that the recognition was at first uncanny); her strong embrace with its radiant warmth; her energetic spirit that has the power to light up my day. Even her stubbornness and impatience are, admittedly, so much like my own.

During my career-oriented life, I was busy developing my own identity still and hadn't taken the time to reflect upon Erica's incalculable value to me. Until then, my compliments had been delivered automatically, because I hadn't paused to appreciate their meaning. It wasn't a matter of neglect, for I was surely a "good mother" in attending to Erica's needs. It was more that I hadn't fully comprehended the magnitude of my role. When my daughter was young, I used to say that we were the best of friends. In so many ways, we were indeed very close. But, too often, a playful atmosphere skirted deeper concerns.

As a career woman, I'd tried to be so very different from my own full-time homemaking mother, and to give my daughter the kind of unchecked independence during her childhood that I hadn't experienced in my own. But I was on unsure ground with my struggling definition of mothering and I failed to offer enough of the limiting guidance that had, in retrospect, been my childhood safety net.

Once my best friend dragged her four-year-old daughter, kicking and screaming, to a salon for a proper haircut. My own daughter's insistence on long hair, with bangs that actually blocked her vision, was driving me to distraction. My exasperated friend took one look at the situation and exclaimed: "But why do you give her so much choice?" Years later, it struck me that I'd given my daughter so much freedom of choice that she'd left without giving an explanation—or, at least, an explanation that made sense to me. Clearly, it was my time for reflection.

During this time, my mother became the wise link between us, the loving center whose fairness provided needed balance to both sides of the coin. One day, a small box arrived in the mail, sent by my mother and her sister, who'd been shopping together. Inside was a small chalkboard—a tacky kitchen souvenir with a red satin ribbon for hanging. On the chalkboard was written: RAISING CHILDREN IS LIKE BEING PECKED TO DEATH BY CHICKENS. This shared sentiment, with all its shameless humor, gave me the hope and the laughter I needed to get on with my life and let my daughter get on with hers. I think this sort of moment is called letting go.

Early one evening I was only a quick lipstick application away from being out the door and off to a party when the phone rang and my world turned on a dime. "Possible appendicitis," stated a doctor's composed voice at the other end of the line. In moments, I was in a taxi, headed to a New York hospital and to my daughter. I charged through the emergency room, dodging gurneys and scanning every face for hers. I was an Amazon mother in search of her child; I was my own mother flinging the bad camp mattresses aside. Time stands still in such a sterile environment; the fragility of life surrounds you. I found my daughter, pale and frightened. But she had become an independent woman, no longer the petulant child who had gone away. "I need my mommy," she cried all the same, her arms outstretched and beckoning. "And your mother needs you!" I cried, flying to her.

Erica and I are rebuilding now, taking care where we were once careless; listening to the spaces between words; reading the language of a look or a sign; and seldom allowing an uncomfortable moment to fester. To my delight, Erica has begun to enjoy modern art, always my exclusive turf in the past. Now it's something we share. During our time apart, my wardrobe had grown dull without her stylish advice. Now it's getting trendier by the season. When I pick up the phone to say: "Just thought I'd give you a quick call," now it's my busy career-woman daughter who declares: "Gotta get back to you later, Mom!"

My mother and I laugh a lot more together these days—most recently, about the time she and I were so busy talking that we never noticed that the car in the parking space we were waiting for was being hot-wired and stolen from the shopping mall garage while we idled there. We even congratulated each other about spotting a place so close to the elevators—a mother and daughter about to do a little shopping

Mother with Erica in 1972.

together, so let those men do what they will! I remember that Mother waved a gracious thank you as two edgy-looking characters backed out, then floored the accelerator and sped from the garage.

Today, I pay more attention to the seemingly insignificant connections among us. For example, it amuses me that a curious little money tradition, begun many years ago by Nanny for me, continues with Mother and Erica. Now it's Erica who looks forward to finding small gifts of money from *her* grandmother—rarely more than a dollar or two—tucked into letters and always wrapped neatly in tin foil or plastic wrap. (In a pinch or a hurry, newsprint.) The wrapping dates back to the days when my grandmother sent "a little something" in her letters to me, camouflaged this way. For the decorous women in our family, something as tacky as cash requires some form of gift wrapping, no matter how modest or casual.

I smile always when I think of these tokens, appreciating that this is but one of many small ways that mother/daughter patterns are passed on through generations of women. At the onset, I may have begun *Mother and Daughter Reflections* for personal reasons; however, it soon expanded into an affirmation of every woman's first significant bond, with its capacity to shape us throughout our lives.

PART ONE

The Gift of a Daughter

Ring out, wild bells—and tame ones, too—
　　Ring out the lover's moon,
Ring in the little worsted socks,
　　Ring in the bib and spoon.
Ring out the muse, ring in the nurse,
　　Ring in the milk and water;
Away with paper, pen and ink—
　　My daughter, oh, my daughter!

--〜 Anonymous,
1905

*M*aking *the decision* to have
a child—it's momentous.
It is to decide forever to have your heart
go walking outside your body.

‒‒ELIZABETH STONE,
1985

(Right) Helen Atsides, who gave birth
to a daughter, Stephanie, in 1947.

She seems to me so fragile that I want to put out my hand to save her from a wrong step, or a careless movement; and at the same time so strong that she is immortal.

~ DORIS LESSING,
1962

eople say you forget the pain and they're
right, but you remember other things so
vividly. A certain look, some offhand comment that is
caught in your memory because your senses are so keen at
that moment, so ready to devour everything. I remember
there in the delivery room, the doctor told me you were
going to be a pianist because you had such long, narrow
fingers. He probably said that to half the mothers. It was
something nice to say. But I remember it, not so much
because your grandmother's family is so talented as
because he was confirming something I already knew to be
true. You could be someone special. I knew you could do
something marvelous, something extraordinary. I willed
that on you the moment you were born.

—Sue Ellen Bridgers,
1981

In the sheltered simplicity of the first days after a baby is born, once sees again the magical closed circle, the miraculous sense of two people existing only for each other, the tranquil sky reflected on the face of the mother nursing her child.

— Anne Morrow Lindbergh,
1955

For the baby, the world is in a state of agreeable expansion: new shapes, new comforts, new warmths. For the mother, the world contracts violently, almost to crib size, and it becomes portable and domestic: bath, formula and blanket. A miracle has come to pass, and lo, it has a schedule.

— B. J. CHUTE, 1957

Pooh—men!
We are done with them now,
Who had need of them, then,
I and you!

—~ Florence Kiper Frank,
1925

I *know her face by heart.* Sometimes I think nothing will break her spell.

—Daphne Merkin, 1986

*T*here are physical mothers and there are spiritual mothers, and there are those who combine the two.

— ELIZABETH HARRISON, 1905

What do you do *with mother love* and wit when the babies are grown and gone away?

~ JOANNE GREENBERG,
1981

Jotted on the back of the snapshot in a fine hand: "Taken last October, but she hasn't changed much other than being heavier and more hair. In the picture she is yelling at a couple of strangers across the street."

She looks to her daughters to carry out some of her own unexpressed ambitions and unlived dreams not easily achieved in her generation of women or within the realm of choices available to her. There is a feeling that her daughter carries on her own personal female spirit.

~ JEANNE KIENZLE,
1999

My mama had a dancing heart
and she shared that heart with me.
With a grin and a giggle,
a hug and a whistle,
we'd slap our knees and mama would say:
"Bless the world
it feels like
a tip-tapping
song singing
finger snapping kind of day.
Let's celebrate!"
And so we did.

~ LIBBA MOORE GRAY,
1995

*M*other's Day will stop being the day you remember to send flowers to your mother; someday the little creature in the crib will come home from kindergarten with enormous pride bringing you a grimy tattered drawing of a flower or a bird or a rabbit on which is written in erratic print: I LOVE MOTHER. That's when you find out why it's called Mother's Day.

—SHIRLEY JACKSON,
1960

Photo: Shirley Zeiberg

*M*others *have need* of sharp eyes and discreet tongues when they have girls to manage.

~ Louisa May Alcott,
1869

Dear Mother your sweet as can be We shore now that.
your lovely and beautiful all over yourself, in goldin light that Is how sweet you are
your Charmin Voic Is beuhful and gay. youl Were a gound prettyer than ever
your nicer than eny Mother oh'oh! yes you are so sweet oh!yes
youd Brack My heart if you left me all allon in the world yes you
Would. your softer then a mink coat yes! yes! yes! yes!
36-37 but you seem to be a lot yongel like 20 or 19'even yes you do
HAPPY Birthday to yOu My Dear mother
    your a tulup   From Lisa
                    to mother

—LEISA CRANE,
1967

The photographer's stamp on the back of the portrait indicates that it was made by Julian Rose Photo Service in Brooklyn, New York.

We are all mothers in special ways. Godmothers, big sisters, aunts, or simply friends with children. There are so many children already here who need love—it isn't necessary to be a mother to experience mothering.

—SARK,
1997

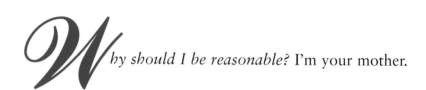

Why should I be reasonable? I'm your mother.

—LYNNE ALPERN AND ESTHER BLUMENFELD,
1986

Photo: Shirley Zeiberg

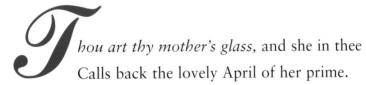

*T*hou art thy mother's glass, and she in thee
Calls back the lovely April of her prime.

~ WILLIAM SHAKESPEARE,
1609

"*Maternal love*," like an orange tree, buds and blossoms and bears at once.

—KATE D. WIGGINS,
1856–1923

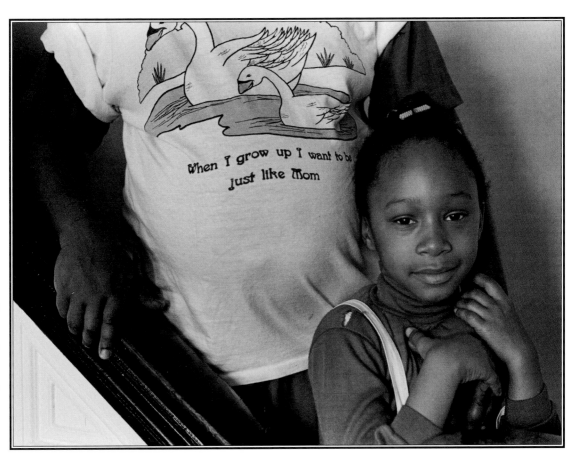

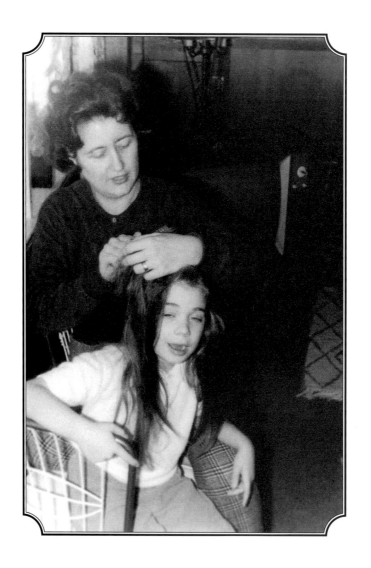

*M*ary Jane says: "This photo is the essence of our relationship."

Mary Jane's mother says: "My daughter's hair is the bane of my existence."

Elizabeth (Betty) Gore and Mary Jane Gore in 1964, when Mary Jane was six years old.

I had the most satisfactory of childhoods
because Mother, small, delicate-boned,
witty and articulate, turned out to be exactly my age.

— KAY BOYLE,
1902–1992

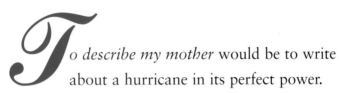

o *describe my mother* would be to write about a hurricane in its perfect power.

--~ MAYA ANGELOU,
1970

PART TWO

The Mirror Image

The older I get, the more of my mother I see in myself. The more opposite my life and thinking grow from hers, the more of her I hear in my voice, see in my facial expression, feel in the emotional reactions I have come to recognize as my own. It is almost as if in extending myself, the circle closes to completion. To say her image is not still a touchstone in my life—and mine in hers— would be another lie.

—NANCY FRIDAY, 1977

It was such an odd thing, motherhood. She didn't understand how people could say, "She's a good mother," in the same way they said, "She's a good neurosurgeon," or "She sings well." It wasn't a skill; there was no past practice to be consulted and perfected by strict application and attention to detail; there was no wisdom you could turn to; every history was inadequate, for each new case was fresh. . . .

—MARY GORDON,
1985

*Y*ou *bring up your girls* as if they
were meant for sideboard
ornaments; and then complain of their frivolity.

–~ Ruskin,
1882

*Y*ou *don't need any advice* on how to be happy at home if you're lucky enough to be the Domestic Type and really like being tied down while one baby yammers to escape from the play pen and Little Sister is still in the layette stage. But if you sometimes get low over being a prisoner in your own home, there's one sure way to keep your spirits from sagging to your ankles.

Look your best. Keep your lipstick on, and your hair, as well as your chin, up. This is easier said than done, especially if you are responsible for the family's cooking, washing, marketing, and that dear, dead, blown-out fuse. But—for a change—let the baby yell for a few minutes while you fix your face and hair, even if you have to turn on the radio to save your nerves.

— MARGARET FISHBACK,
1945

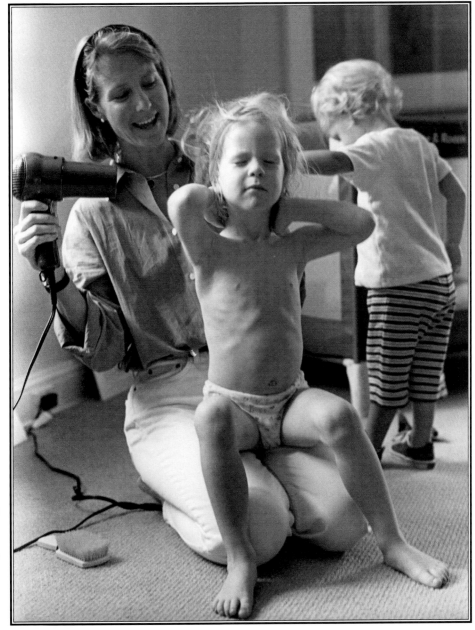

My mother was dressed in her beautiful yellow summer robe, the tie cinched evenly into a bow at the exact center of her waist, but her auburn hair was sticking up in the back, an occasional occurrence that I always hated seeing, since in my mind it suggested a kind of incompetence. It was an unruly cowlick, nearly impossible to tame—I knew this, having an identical cowlick of my own . . . but I did not forgive its presence on my mother.

~ Elizabeth Berg,
1998

In the early morning
　　I shake my head
to clear away the static
of the dream
the way my daughter
shakes the radio she holds
against her ear
as if it were a shell.
On the table between us
the sun spreads
its slow stain;
fog lifts
from the coffee;
a heart drifts out of reach
on the surface
of the milk.
Now my daughter takes the day
into her hand
like a fresh-baked bread—
she offers me a piece.

—LINDA PASTAN,
1980

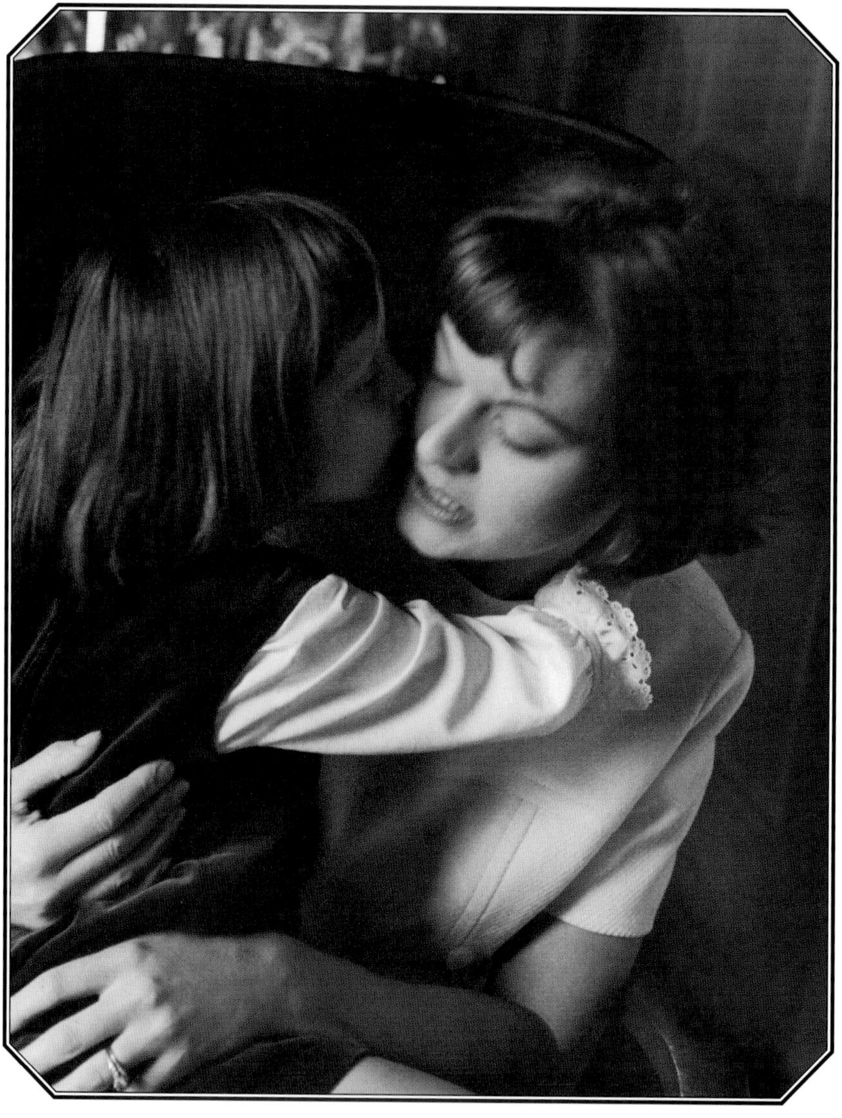

Photo: Shirley Zeiberg

A girl cannot go along motherless without life's noticing, taking a compensatory tuck here and there in the heart and in the mind, letting out one seam or another whenever she is threatened by her loneliness.

—KAYE GIBBONS,
1995

*I*f *you've ever had a mother* and if she's given you and meant to you all the things you care for most, you never get over it.

~ ANNE DOUGLAS SEDGEWICK,
1929

I learned *your walk,* talk, gestures and nurturing laughter. At that time, Mama, had you swung from bars, I would, to this day, be hopelessly, imitatively, hung up.

— SDIANE BOGUS,
1977

Wendy Wood and her daughter, eight-year-old Courtney

I cannot forget my mother. Though not as sturdy as others, she is my bridge. When I needed to get across, she steadied herself long enough for me to run across safely.

—RENITA WEEMS,
1991

*I*f I could have given birth to you,
   I would have. I would have taken you
inside me, held you
and given birth to you again.
I like to think that wherever you go, you will
keep some memory of sunlight in the room
where I first loved you, and you first loved.

— FRAN CASTAN,
1986

*R*emember that Saturday morning
Mother forgot the word gull?

We were all awake, but still in bed
and she called out, "Hey kids!

What's the name of that bird that eats garbage
and stands around in cold water on the beach?"

And you, the quick one, the youngest daughter,
piped right back: "A dirty-billed freeze footy!"

And she laughed till she was weak,
until it hurt her. And you had done it:
reduced was our queen to warm and helpless rubble.

And the rest of the day, baking or cleaning
or washing our hair until it squeaked,
whenever she caught sight of you
it would start all over again.

~ JUDITH HEMSCHEMEYER,
1975

People think I'm wild and queer, but Mother understands and helps me. I have not told anyone about my plan; but I'm going to *be* good. I've made so many resolutions, and written sad notes, and cried over my sins, and it doesn't seem to do any good! Now I'm going to *work really,* for I feel a true desire to improve, and be a help and comfort, not a care and sorrow, to my dear mother.

~Louisa May Alcott,
1846

I *am sure that there were times* when my mother did not know whence the next week's food would come. One can understand how this struggle would have affected her attitude toward her daughters, even if her previous life had not shown her aversion to dependency. She fed our ambitions.

~ SUE SHELDON WHITE,
1926

All daughters, even when most aggravated by their mothers, have a secret respect for them. They believe perhaps that they can do everything better than their mothers can, and many things they *can* do better, but they have not yet lived long enough to be sure how successfully they will meet the major emergencies of life, which lie, sometimes quite creditably, *behind* their mothers.

~ PHYLLIS BOTTOME,
1943

She grieved when we told lies. She talked to us about turning the other cheek and sometimes for love of her we tried this experiment. Once I asked her if I could ever be beautiful like my lovely sister, and she said I could not because my eyes, my hair, my skin would never equal Jane's. I could, however, be remarkable for goodness.

~ VICTORIA MCALMON,
1926

*A*nd *you reach out* to hold on to your child and she is slipping away, going off into some life that is not your life, and you are afraid to see her go because you know, you know how far it is possible to let things slip away.

— KELLY CHERRY,
1993

We are, none of us, either mothers
or daughters; to our amazement,
confusion, and greater complexity, we are both.

— SIV CEDERING,
1976

*M*other *and I* would get into a battle of wills at the drop of a hat, especially when push came to shove. And, over the years, we had our share of pushing and shoving. Yet, months after she died, I'd find myself reaching for the phone to call her each night at our usual time. I miss our routine.

—Anonymous

As angry as she was with her mother, there were times when she'd awaken in the night out of some groping dream of displacement, and it would be her mother's face that would comfort her. Memories would flood over her—the two of them at the beach climbing dunes of burning sand, forcing each other to the summit because neither of them would give up; the kitchen table splattered with finger paint or pails of colored water for her to play in; bits of yarn and dogwood branches for branch weaving; her mother at the piano studying the notes with fierce concentration as she accompanied Ellery's flute; a book left on her dresser that turned out to be just what Ellery needed to read, as if Ginny knew her readiness before she did. Ginny teaching her how to stuff a leg of lamb, how to slice potatoes paper thin, how to make a pot of soup out of leftovers and a skinny chicken. Practical things.

— SUE ELLEN BRIDGERS,
1987

A daughter looking at her mother's life is looking at her own, shaping and fitting one life to suit the needs of another. Some have shaped monsters and some angels. Most who make angels see their mothers as the sources of art, the tree of creative life. We need to do this. We have always needed to do this.

~ LOUISE BERNIKOW,
1980

*B*etween *these two* there was no generation gap, no chasm. My mother never wracked her brain explaining why she and her mother couldn't "relate" . . . Far from dreading her visits—as so many women I know secretly dread their mothers' visits—my mother looked forward to being under the same roof with her. "Mama is coming to stay with us for a while" was a boast, not the presentiment of a nervous breakdown.

—SHIRLEY ABBOTT,
1983

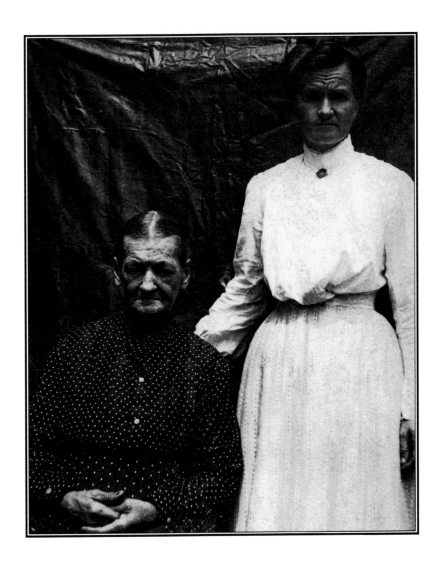

PART THREE

The Legacy

She belongs not just to me but to all the women who preceded her. Another daughter born into this chain of mothers. Sometimes I look at her upturned face, her smile so quick and so earnest, her eyes locked so intently on mine, and I think, Here is where it begins. One generation at a time.

— HOPE EDELMAN,
1999

I long to *put the experience* of fifty years at once into your young lives, to give you at once the key of that treasure chamber every gem of which has cost me tears and struggles and prayers, but you must work for these inward treasures yourselves.

—Harriet Beecher Stowe, 1861

Violet Cavoulas with three of her granddaughters—
Stephanie, Valerie, and Joanne—in 1949.

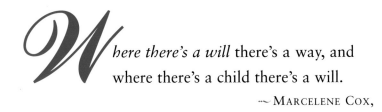

*W*here *there's a will* there's a way, and
where there's a child there's a will.

— MARCELENE COX,
1950

Your child will be a	If you give it
Architect	Cottage pudding
Baseball Player	Any good batter
Chiropodist	Corn
Electrician	Currants
Historian	Dates
Lawyer	Suet
Musician	Hominy
Parisienne Cloak Model	French dressing
Politician	Tongue
Postman	Lettuce
Prize Fighter	Punch
Plumber	Leeks
Sailor	Roe
Shoemaker	Sole and eel or any good cobbler
Stock Broker	Succotash
Subway Guard	Jam and squash
Surgeon	Caviar

~ JEROME S. MEYER,
1927

Leisa Crane, age one, with her grandmother,
Elizabeth "Beta" Suhayda, in 1961.

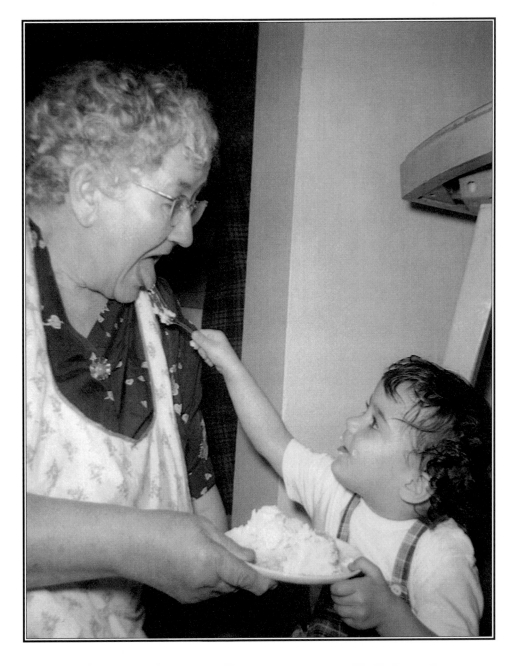

*W*omen *who outlive* their
daughters are orphans,
Abuela tells me. Only their granddaughters
can save them, guard their knowledge like
the first fire.

—⁓ CRISTINA GARCIA,
1992

One could not live without delicacy, but when
I think of love I think of the big, clumsy-looking
hands of my grandmother, each knuckle a knob.

～ Mona Van Duyn,
1990

Grandma was a kind of first-aid station, or a Red Cross nurse, who took up where the battle ended, accepting us and our little sobbing sins, gathering the whole of us into her lap, restoring us to health and confidence by her amazing faith in life and in a mortal's strength to meet it.

~ LILLIAN SMITH,
1954

Grandma . . . had a great deal to do
with the education of her
granddaughters. In general she not so much
trained as just shed herself upon us.

—BERTHA DAMON,
1938

*O*ur mythology tells us so much about fathers and sons. . . . What do we know about mothers and daughters? . . . Our power is so oblique, so hidden, so ethereal a matter, that we rarely struggle with our daughters over actual kingdoms or corporate shares. On the other hand, our attractiveness dries as theirs blossoms, our journey shortens just as theirs begins. We too must be afraid and awed and amazed that we cannot live forever and that our replacements are eager for their turn, indifferent to our wishes, ready to leave us behind.

— ANNE ROIPHE,
1987

Hilda Effania was ecstatic. All her girls were home. Cypress was back from studying dance in New York. Sassafrass had made that terrible bus trip from New England. As much as they'd changed she still recognized them as her children. Spinning in the kitchen, while the girls did whatever they were going to do, was her most precious time.

~ NTOZAKE SHANGE,
1982

Whenever I'm with my mother, I feel as though I have to spend the whole time avoiding land mines.

~ AMY TAN,
1991

*H*er grandmother, as she
gets older, is not fading
but rather becoming more concentrated.

— PAULETTE BATES ALDEN,
1988

*S*ara loved receiving such a flood of attention from her overwhelming, wonderful mother, and together mother and daughter developed an alliance: the big and the small, the formed and the unformed. They sang songs, they paged through fashion magazines, they once even bleached their hair with temporary dye, transforming themselves into mother-daughter platinum-blond starlets for one night only. Each received a borrowed burst of voltage from the other, the appropriation of qualities that would otherwise never be available.

--- MEG WOLITZER,
1999

*T*he women of today are the thoughts of their mothers and grandmothers, embodied, and made alive. They are active, capable, determined and bound to win. They have one thousand generations back of them. . . . Millions of women, dead and gone, are speaking through us today.

—MATILDA JOSLYN GAGE,
1889

*W*hen three generations are
present in a family, one of
them is bound to be revolutionary.

― ELISE BOULDING,
1978

Even feminist mothers for whom the subject of motherhood is a passion seldom write candidly about it except abstractly or from the point of view of the daughter. This leaves a great hole in our knowledge that few are willing to fill. Certainly not I. Though the subject of my life as a mother could be another chapter in this book, like my own mother, I remain silent.

—ALIX KATES SHULMAN,
1999

Acknowledgments

O*nce again, I relied on the keen insights* of my friend and researcher, Leisa Crane, to help me sort through countless words and images for the right combinations. Exploring individual works as well as splendid anthologies on the topics of women and motherhood, we found an amazing body of work from which to draw the text for *Mother and Daughter Reflections*. Many of the women writers quoted in this book have written on the theme of mothers and daughters in more than one of their works and are worth exploring.

In addition to the usual research, we drew from a sustaining network of women friends and colleagues who are writers. Having acted as her editor during my years in publishing, I will admit a special fondness for mother/daughter relationships in the young adult books of Sue Ellen Bridgers—especially *Notes for Another Life* and *Permanent Connections*. I am also indebted to Alix Kates Shulman, whose recently published memoir, *A Good Enough Daughter,* provides a poignant and fitting text on which to end this book. Thanks also to friend and writer Louise Bernikow for the use of her insightful words from her book, *Among Women.* Many women friends talked with me in informal interviews about their mothers and daughters and include my sister, Jeanne Kienzle, Alix Lynch, and Nancy Hays.

It was a pleasure to return to many of the photographers who contributed to the previous photographic anthologies to find so many new and poignant images. My sincere appreciation to Sandra Weiner, for her work and for Dan Weiner's; David Graham; Karen Woodard; and Mary Motley Kalergis. Thanks for the third time to photo researcher Gillian Speeth, who brought Shirley Zeiberg's many thoughtful images to our attention. Also, thanks to Fern Richman for her discerning eye.

In terms of all the wonderful and capable people at Andrews McMeel, the first thing that springs to mind is: Once more with feeling. Special thanks to Christine Schillig, my editor; Jean Zevnik, who so capably shepherded this project from the start; Holly Camerlinck, who put her own artful stamp on Virginia Norey's original design for these books; Katie Mace and Tamara Haus, who oversaw the many stages of production; and Kathy Viele in subsidiary rights, who got the word out.

As always, many friends sorted through their photo albums to find possible images for this book. Thanks to Carolyn Gore-Ashe, Mary Jane Gore, and Elizabeth Gore; also Marylin Hafner, Joan Suyhada, and Jane Bergere. My love always to my mother, Anita Kienzle, and to my daughter, Erica Ross, for their constant support on this heartfelt project.

Credits

The following photographs, indicated by the page on which they appear, have been printed with permission: ii, 80: photo by Dan Weiner, courtesy Sandra Weiner; dedication page: photo by Arthur Hartog, courtesy Fay Hartog; preface and pages xx, 2, 4, 7, 8, 12, 15, 16, 19, 20, 23, 29, 30, 44, 47, 48, 49, 52, 59, 62, 65, 69, 70, 73, 75, 76, 79, 83, 84, 87, 92, 96, 98, 101, 102, 105, 106, 109, 110, 113, 114, 118, and 123: photo collection of Pat Ross; pages 3, 91, and 95: courtesy Leisa Crane; page 11: photo by David Graham, courtesy David Graham; page 25: photo by Karen Woodard, courtesy Karen Woodard; pages 26, 33, 34, 51, 56, 66, and 117: photos by Shirley Zeiberg, courtesy Shirley Zeiberg; pages 37 and 88: photos copyright Mary Motley Kalergis, courtesy Mary Motley Kalergis; page 38: courtesy Elizabeth Gore; page 41: Urban Archives, Temple University, Philadelphia, Pa.; page 42: photo by Sandra Weiner, courtesy Sandra Weiner; page 55: Archive Photos; page 61: photo by Tom Rykoff, courtesy Tom Rykoff.

The following text has been used by permission: page 22: from *My Mama Had A Dancing Heart* by Libba Moore Gray, illustrated by Rául Colón. Text copyright © 1995 by Libba

About the Author

Pat Ross is the author of many popular books that relate to the theme of home—specifically design, entertaining, and gardening—as well as titles dealing with women's issues, including *The Kinship of Women* and *The Circle of Enduring Love,* and the humor books *Menopause Madness* and *Men Exposed.* Her lifestyle books include *Formal Country* (recently reissued in a tenth anniversary edition), three titles in the Country Cupboard series (*Flowers, Kitchens,* and *Herbs*), as well as two garden books—*Decorating Your Garden* and the recently published *A Ceiling of Sky,* both of which feature the author's own photographs. Pat Ross began collecting early photographs a number of years ago when she renewed a longtime interest in photography.

For many years, Pat Ross owned Sweet Nellie, a popular and trendsetting Madison Avenue shop that specialized American crafts and designs for the home. Now she writes full-time from her home in New York City and a farm in McDowell, Virginia.